BLACKPINK

A Little Golden Book® Biography

By Jessica Yoon • Illustrated by Honee Jang

For Luna, Talia, Daniella, Ada, and Ellie—my favorite BLINKs
— J.Y.

 A GOLDEN BOOK • NEW YORK

Golden Books
An imprint of Random House Children's Books
A division of Penguin Random House LLC
1745 Broadway, New York, NY 10019
penguinrandomhouse.com
rhcbooks.com
Text copyright © 2025 by Jessica Yoon
Cover art and interior illustrations copyright © 2025 by Honee Jang
Golden Books, A Golden Book, A Little Golden Book, the G colophon, and the
distinctive gold spine are registered trademarks of Penguin Random House LLC.
Library of Congress Control Number: 2025934116
ISBN 979-8-217-12360-5 (trade) — ISBN 979-8-217-12361-2 (ebook)
Manufactured in the United States of America
10 9 8 7 6 5 4 3 2 1
EU Contact: Penguin Random House Ireland, 32 Nassau Street, Dublin D02 YH68.
https://eu-contact.penguin.ie

BLACKPINK, the iconic K-pop group featuring Jisoo, Jennie, Rosé, and Lisa, has been releasing hit songs since 2016. The band was formed in South Korea by YG Entertainment and went on to become the biggest girl group in the world. Fans everywhere love their music, their dancing, and their catchphrase: "BLACKPINK in your area!"

Kim Ji-soo, who goes by Jisoo, was born on January 3, 1995. She grew up outside of Seoul, South Korea, with her parents, older brother and sister, and grandparents. As a child, Jisoo wanted to be a writer or painter.

In eleventh grade, Jisoo joined her school's drama club and decided to become an actor instead. She thought going on auditions would be a good way to gain experience. Her very first audition was for YG's K-pop idol training program. Jisoo was shocked when she was accepted as a trainee!

Jennie Kim, known simply as Jennie, was born in Korea on January 16, 1996. When she was eight years old, she went on a family vacation to New Zealand. Her mom wanted her to experience different cultures, so she asked Jennie if she'd like to live there. Jennie said yes!

She moved to New Zealand when she was ten and lived with a local family while attending school and learning English. This experience helped her to become independent from a young age.

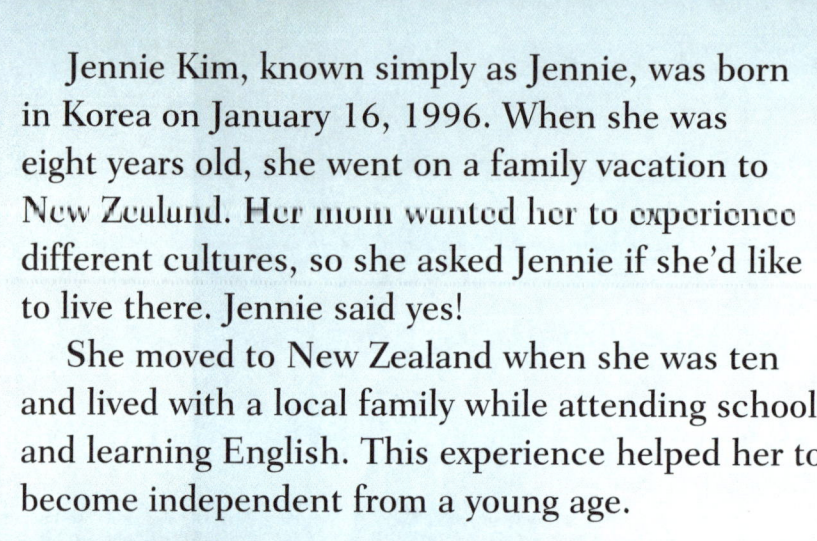

Jennie was a big fan of K-pop and returned to Korea at age fourteen to pursue a singing career. In 2010, she began training with YG.

Roseanne Chae-young Park, better known as Rosé (or Rosie to her friends and family), was born on February 11, 1997, in New Zealand. She moved to Australia with her parents and older sister when she was eight years old.

As a kid, Rosé played the guitar and sang in her church choir. She spent so much time at the piano that she sometimes fell asleep there!

Rosé's dad recognized her musical talent. In 2012, he flew her from Melbourne to Sydney to audition for YG. She came in first place out of seven hundred applicants! At age fifteen, Rosé left school and moved to Korea to begin training.

Lalisa Manobal, who uses the stage name Lisa, was born on March 27, 1997, in Thailand. She started taking dance lessons in kindergarten, and soon she was entering dance competitions.

When Lisa was around thirteen years old, a talent scout saw her perform and suggested she also try singing. This inspired Lisa to audition for YG. Out of four thousand Thai applicants, she was the only one accepted. When she moved to Korea for training, she didn't know the language. Now Lisa speaks Korean, English, and basic Mandarin and Japanese in addition to Thai.

Training was difficult. The girls often worked fourteen hours a day, with only one day off every two weeks. They took singing and rapping lessons. They practiced many styles of dance—everything from ballet to hip-hop. They also studied languages and learned interview skills to prepare them for their future as celebrities.

One thing that made training easier was the friendships the girls formed. Jennie and Lisa first bonded as the only two English-speaking trainees. Later, when Rosé joined the program, she and Lisa connected over being from other countries. They spent so much time together that Lisa started speaking with an Australian accent! As the oldest in the group, Jisoo acted as the group's unnie, which is Korean for "older sister," and did her best to take care of the other girls.

BLACKPINK

RAPPER

DANCER

After years of training, Jennie, Jisoo, Lisa, and Rosé were selected to be in BLACKPINK! Jennie was the main rapper and Lisa was the main dancer, while Rosé and Jisoo focused on vocals. All four girls were like the colors in their group's name—feminine like the color pink and confident like the color black.

VOCALS

On August 8, 2016, BLACKPINK released their first record, a two-track album called *Square One*. The songs "휘파람 (Whistle)" and "붐바야 (Boombayah)" were instant hits! Within two weeks of debut, BLACKPINK performed both songs live on the Korean TV show *Inkigayo* and won first place for most popular song!

In 2018, they starred in their first reality series called *BLACKPINK House*. The girls, plus Jisoo's dog Dalgom and Jennie's dog Kuma, were filmed living together in a pink house for one hundred days. Their fans, known as BLINKs, loved getting to know the girls' personalities better as they watched them do everyday activities like cooking, cleaning, and shopping.

The girls practiced hard to learn dance routines for their songs. In addition to making music videos, they also made dance performance videos that showed off their awesome moves. Their videos continue to be loved by BLINKs and have broken world records for number of views on YouTube.

In 2019, BLACKPINK became the first female K-pop group to perform at the Coachella Music Festival. They sang hits like "뚜두뚜두 (Ddu-Du Ddu-Du)" and "Kill This Love" in front of thousands of fans. The girls couldn't believe that so many people had traveled to California to see them—and to sing along in Korean!

BLACKPINK was proud to share Korean language and culture with BLINKs around the world. Most of their song lyrics are in Korean. The girls also wore modern versions of traditional Korean clothing called the hanbok in their "How You Like That" music video.

When they returned to Coachella in 2023, they made history as the first Asian headliners—and their main set was designed to look like a traditional Korean house called a hanok.

BLACKPINK has used their fame to let people around the world know how important it is to protect the environment. They were named Advocates of the United Nations Climate Change Conference (COP26). For their years of good work, they were invited to dinner at Buckingham Palace in England. Each of them wore a gown fit for royalty. During their visit, they were also named honorary Members of the Order of the British Empire. They wore stylish suits to receive this honor.

The girls enjoy expressing themselves through fashion, and they each have their own unique style. Fashion companies love working with them because they are trendsetters. In fact, there were times clothes have sold out just because the BLACKPINK girls wore them!

While the girls of BLACKPINK love performing as a group, they have also had success with solo projects.

Rosé released the super-catchy song "APT." with Bruno Mars It has more than one billion views on YouTube!

Jennie's hit song "Like Jennie" featured her impressive Korean and English rap skills and became a viral dance challenge!

Jisoo starred in the historical K-drama *Snowdrop* as well as the zombie comedy series *Newtopia*.

Lisa acted in the third season of *The White Lotus*, which was filmed in Thailand. She was very excited to return to her home country for this project!

Jisoo, Jennie, Rosé, and Lisa's hard work and talents helped them become global superstars. But it's their love and support for one another that made it possible for them to get through years of training and keep following their dreams. As they look toward the future, one thing is certain— on stage or on the screen, apart or together, BLACKPINK will light up the sky!